Today I

Saw the

Mountains

A Story of Overcoming

Obsessive Compulsive

Disorder

Allison Porto

Order this book online at www.trafford.com
or email orders@trafford.com

Most Trafford titles are also available at major online book retailers.

Printed in the United States of America.

ISBN: 978-1-5536-9284-3 (SC)

Trafford rev. 11/18/2011

 www.trafford.com

North America & international
toll-free: 1 888 232 4444 (USA & Canada)
phone: 250 383 6864 ♦ fax: 812 355 4082

For Beth

With Love

Special thanks to my mother, father, sister, family, and friends for their constant support and love. Thanks to Chris and Maria Kimball who helped make this book possible and to my teacher and mentor, Meghan Thorpe who believed that someday I would be a writer.

There are so many people who have
supported me in my decision to write and
publish this book. I would like to take this
time to thank all these wonderful people:
June Clausen, Anne DeBenedict, Jim and
Dorothy Devitt, Julia Hill, William Murphy,
Jim Murphy, Al Porto, Eileen Porto, Erin
Turner and all others whose support has
meant so much to me.

In Loving Memory Of

William "Billy" Murphy

1948-1983

I love you Uncle Billy. You are my inspiration.

Preface

Trapped. Confused. Alone. My name is Allie, welcome to my world. This is the world of Obsessive Compulsive Disorder. It is a strange world, one that I've been trapped in ever since I was a little girl and one that you will never truly understand unless you are in it. But there are some things you can know. There are things that can make you more aware of what people afflicted with this disorder are going through every moment of their lives. But you can help. In fact, I need you. I need you to help me. You can do it by just reading my book.

Spreading awareness of this disorder

can help those that are not seeking treatment

because they don't know what is wrong with

them. It can help parents recognize the

problems their children are facing, and it

might even help you. There are so many

people out there who have Obsessive

Compulsive Disorder (OCD) but are afraid to

get help. Society recognizes this disorder as

something that one should be ashamed of but

that's not true. It's not something that makes

you a bad person. It just makes you different

and different is not bad. In fact, this disorder

is pretty common; more common then you think. People think that only "freaks" have it, but that is the furthest thing from the truth. People are afraid of what they do not know and cannot explain. Maybe if they are educated about this disorder they will someday understand that people with OCD are people just like them. So thanks for helping me spread the word. If we can help just one person it is all worth it.

The Killer Routine

Chapter One

"Allie, wake up. Rise and shine." The sound of my mother's voice echoed in and out of my ears each morning. Although it seemed cheerful, I dreaded to hear those words, for it meant I would actually have to get myself out of bed and go to school. "Allie is definitely not a morning person," my aunt would say. And it was so true. More so than ever. I simply couldn't stand the fact that I actually was forced to get out from beneath my warm covers and uncurl myself from the lovely ball position I had slept in. I didn't even want to think about walking along the frozen hardwood floors to the shower where I would encounter temporary warmth. The whole morning was annoying. I just wanted to sleep and would rather not face another day.

That just seemed to be my mind set. There was the positive and there was the negative. Most of the time the negative consumed my thoughts. It seemed to be such a persistent force. But despite it all, tired and cold, I dragged myself out of bed each morning and started my journey for the long day ahead.

I traveled onward to school, a Catholic one that I attended about thirty minutes or so from my house. I carpooled with the same guy who had been my friend since pre-school. Sleepy and on the shy side, he would be there every morning awaiting me at the front door. As I stepped into his giant, tan-colored van I liked to call "The Bus" I would move to my seat in the back. I usually crashed over the sticky dishes that once held waffles or pancakes, even the occasional scrambled eggs. The drive to school with his mom was always a "kick in the pants." She was a driving maniac. She took us through all the back roads to avoid the traffic but they ended up taking twice as long and made us all carsick.

My friends crooked smile and naïve attitude never failed me. I would look out the windows and see the passing cars and the trees and all of nature. I learned to appreciate nature at such a young age because it was something that seemed to fill the voids in my life. Not that I was really lacking in any way, I just turned to nature to be there for me. I had always thought of it as an escape from the reality that was tearing my life apart. I saw nature as a way to get out and free from

the hell I was in. Nature was beautiful and

bright. It was full of such peace, quite a

difference from my dark, frightful world.

Everyday was a struggle and I constantly

fought with my brain. I could see the world

only through a window with thick blinds.

Those blinds being my OCD and turning all

that my eyes captured into something

horrible.

The day had just begun and the OCD

was persistent as ever. My mind would race

with obsessions of bad thoughts, mostly of

death and commanded my brain to follow the obsessions with mental compulsions. I talked to myself out loud and struggled with strange body movements. IT all seems to be both a blur and a vivid picture as I embarked not only to school but on my long journey with OCD.

A Different Kid

Chapter Two

Why didn't anybody find out sooner?

Wasn't it obvious enough? Of course I didn't

know, but they are adults and they should

have known, right? From the time I was little

I always thought of myself as someone who

was different from everybody else, an

outsider to the "in" crowd and I didn't know

why.

"Weird." The word became all too

familiar to me. I was an eager child, looking

for adventure, but shying away at the

slightest of things too. The oldest of my

family, I stood tall and proud at a young age.

IT was the only time I ever felt that pride. As a child I was well off and lived in a beautiful house in California, a small suburb town about twenty-five miles from San Francisco. As I grew, I looked to "The City" as a place full of life. Later I learned that I was attracted to it because of its variety of people. It was somewhere where I might finally fit in.

My parents could not have been more loving to my sister Kerry and me. They love us more than anything else on Earth. I knew it because they showed it. My parents always told me that actions spoke louder than words and there were right. My first therapist said that there were overprotective, but I think that they are caring.

Although I had friends, I always seemed to be the odd man out. Sure it all started with the innocent teasing at school and all, and that's what kids will do. Little did they know that when you are teased so much, to a degree you actually start believing it.

I did all right at academics. I wasn't the absolute perfect student but poured my heart into my studies and tried the best I could. If there is one thing that I learned from my whole experience with this disease, it is that you cannot give up or you will fail. Sure I had the normal difficulties of a third, fourth, and fifth grader but I got past them and moved on. Of course I never really got past my dilemma with math, but that is a whole other funny story.

I went to a school that required that all the students were uniforms. I didn't really mind it and until this day I could care less if I had to wear a uniform for the rest of my life. I was not really aware of the real reasons for wearing them at the time. However, now I know that no one was ever judged by the way they looked because we all looked the same. I had previously experienced harassment about my weight and my looks and I was thrilled that I didn't have to add my clothes to that list.

Struggles with the Catholic school in my hometown persisted and my parents became very unhappy with it. I did not really know what was going on except for the fact that a bunch of teachers had conspired to fire a principal, who in the eyes of my parents, was a blessing to the school. So I was pulled out after fifth grade. I still recall the last day of school.

A girl had called me up the night before and asked me to go over to her house with a bunch of her friends after school. I was so taken back by this offer because this girl was so popular and pretty and never in my wildest dreams did I think that she would invite me over to her house. So I accepted with awe and climbed into her mom's car and drove to her house the following day.

I remember her living at the top of a huge hill in a beautiful brown house with green trim. After we had arrived, everyone decided to go swimming in her pool. I was so excited because I love swimming and jumped right in. Some of the girls started to make conversation about favorite music groups. Unfortunately, the OCD got in the way of my fun and I guess I appeared strange to them. I felt so compelled to go under the water a particular way for a certain amount of times and felt like I had to say special words to myself to relieve the anxiety I was experiencing. The anxiety had nothing to do with the girls. My mind was simply playing tricks with me. I felt compelled to touch the bottom of the pool with my hands many different times and had to do it while repeating the special phrases and words. This made it very hard to enjoy myself. All I long to do was swim, like normal girls would.

I remember one girl asking me what music group I liked. I felt a bit stuck because I didn't even know much about the popular groups. They had been talking about such groups as New Kids on the Block and billions of others I had never even heard of. The only music I could think of was the songs from Disney movies. Well apparently I should have just agreed with them because the girls gave me these looks of astonishment and starting laughing. I felt so small and so stupid. I hated that feeling so much but it was one I would grow to know quite closely.

Throughout the rest of the day, the girls continued to make fun of me and I ended up wandering around aimlessly trying to keep the tears back. I was simply heart broken at the fact that she only invited me over to poke fun at me. To do this day I often remember that experience and it still makes me sad and angry. I ended up going to high school with that girl and she of course grew to be even more beautiful and popular. I understand that every person gets teased at some point in their life. I know it is not just me and I hate feeling sorry for myself. I just wish it were for other reasons than the OCD.

Rituals

Chapter Three

The word ritual pretty much identifies this whole illness and boy did I have a million of them. In fact I still do. Most of the time people identify this illness with compulsive hand washing or being afraid to step on a crack for fear of breaking a mother's back. Those are compulsive rituals of which I had many. Some included checking rituals like making sure the stove was turned off, or making sure I filled up my dog's water bowl. One time is normal, fifty times is compulsive. These rituals would constantly keep me up late at night.

I used to lie in my bed wondering if I had really turned out the lights in the other room or did I just think I did. I simply did not trust myself. I used to walk a certain way to ensure that nothing bad would happen to the people I loved. I had to get into bed just the right way with exactly three steps just in order to relax.

Getting ready for bed was another story. It took a very long time, sometimes even hours. Everything had to be in the right order. I had to make sure I brushed my teeth and washed my hands many, many times before I could get into bed at all. I always had a glass of water near my bedside because I was always afraid that if I did not drink enough, I would get dehydrated. I used to tough things a thousand different times to make sure something bad wouldn't happen.

These compulsions involved reading and writing as well. I could not get through a page of a book or even a sentence without thinking terrible things. I refused to look at or write the word "death" or any other word I found scary. When those words were spoken or eve read they would trigger rituals that would last for hours. I continued to think if I did not do every step of the ritual right, something would happen.

Those rituals were really hard to stop and I was able to do it with exposure therapy. But the mental rituals were, and still are the hardest to conquer. It has been calculated that I have a mental ritual about three times per minute. Those add up to about fifteen hundred times every twelve hours or so. It is a lot for a person to handle. I could not stop them because they were so relentless. It is all about corresponding the physical compulsions like washing or checking with the mental ones and making sure that both sets of rituals were executed simultaneously.

I had hundreds of phrases sitting in my head that I would used to try to counteract the bad thoughts that shot through my mind. I would say that I did not want bad things to happen to other people and I only wanted good things for them. I wanted all the bad things that I was thinking to happen to me, not ever to them. To reassure myself of this, I repeated my name over and over again.

When I finished a ritual and thought I had it right and could finally relax, I would doubt myself and have to do it over again a hundred times. It was so hard to get everything perfect. In reality, it is nearly impossible for a person to do so many things at the same time. But, I didn't think about it like that. I thought that I just could not do it and so I continued on, hundreds of times each day. I could not make the thoughts go away or stop the compulsions. I was never satisfied, never. Finally I would find a bit of relief, but even then I knew I was not satisfied.

However, this relief was only temporary. I would repeat these acts several times throughout the day and night in an attempt to calm myself. What I did not know was that I was making the "OCD" stronger. I could not trust myself. How could I be thinking these thoughts? There were terrible and I had to make them go away. The compulsions were a temporary way out.

It was quite a relentless process and one that still affects me to this day. The thoughts are strong and have become even

stronger over the years because they have

been reinforced so frequently. I was and still

am so afraid that people will take notice.

Obviously it is not normal behavior and I

know that, but I cannot help what I am doing.

The process is almost instant and the

responses to the triggers are automatic.

I the beginning I was so embarrassed

of what I looked like and afraid of what

people might think or say. Now I just seem so

numb to it. I think to myself that it is my

personal business and it is something that I

have to deal with right now. Worrying about
what other people think of me will not help.

Wondering what people think is
something no person should do whether they
have OCD or not. It is senseless and simply
stressful but it is something we all do. I try to
remember that it is what I think, deep inside
myself that is truly important.

It was not until years later that I
learned these thoughts were lies. The horrible
pictures I form in my mind are not real and I
cannot make them happen by simply thinking
about them. I still have a hard time

convincing myself that the thoughts are false. Sometimes I have really put my foot down and yell back at the "monster" that is feeding my mind these lies. It is a process that is going to take me a long time, but I have faith that I will get there someday. One of these days my mind will be free and in turn, I would have my life back. Many times I am impatient and frustrated and wonder when it will get better. But I try to remember to tell myself that I have worked hard since my initial diagnosis and that it will take a lot more work and time to feel better.

Germs

Chapter Four

Still affected with OCD, I continued right on to junior high where I experienced beautiful friendships that I still hold dear today. But as I grew, the OCD grew and became more prevalent in my actions. I became totally obsessed with germs. I was so afraid of contacting a life-threatening disease such as AIDS or Cancer that I began to wash my hands fifty times a day and take two or three showers to make sure I was absolutely clean. I was afraid of touching people and was petrified of public restrooms because I just "knew" I would get sick from them. As a result of my distorted thinking, my hands became chapped and blistered and people would ask me why they looked so bad. I would say, "Oh it's just the season and they're peeling." What a stupid lie. But my obsessive thoughts were strong and I no longer trusted myself or anyone else. I fed the obsessions and they grew until they took over my entire life. My mind and body were under its control and there was so escaping. I would stay up late into the night, trying to get myself into my bed, but could not without washing my hands a certain number of times or getting in bed and then back out because I thought I was not clean. Many times I became easily frustrated and most nights, after fighting forever, finally gave up and cried myself to sleep, praying that nothing bad would happen.

The summer before my freshman year in high school was slowly passing and I ventured up to Lake Tahoe with my family. It must have been the thirteenth or fourteenth year in a row that we all had been vacationing up there. I was so excited because all my cousins would be there and I could not wait to breathe in that mountain air. I loved the house we stayed in and longed for the warm sand at the beach. Sometimes it felt like home away from home since we stayed for two weeks. The whole gang would play basketball outside at the hoop hovering over the garage.

A distinct recollection of being made fun of because of my disorder was that year in Lake Tahoe. My cousins and I were standing on the steps leading up to the front door and I went into a repetitive motion or said something funny and the reaction hit me hard as a rock. I remember moving my hands in a certain direction and repeating something about God and the stares and laughter broke out with a bang. Of course no one understood that I had a disease and this harmless criticism, if you will, hurt me very much. They laughed and imitated me for the rest of the vacation. I know it was not their fault, they did not know. But I knew there was something wrong with me. I just didn't know what.

I recall another experience that occurred when I was in the restroom in our house in Tahoe.

I would use so many sheets of wet paper towels to clean my hands. After multiple cleanings, I would crumble them up and throw them away in the trash. Little crumbs of the paper towel that did not make it into the wastebasket would end up all over the floor and get stuck in the rug on the bathroom floor. At this point my parents knew that there was something wrong with me but could not figure it out. I was warned to clean it up before people saw and said something to me. Later that day someone did say something and blamed it on my sister. I felt so bad but did not say anything. My sister just swallowed her pride and covered up for

me to save me the embarrassment. That time I
was lucky.

The Beginning of an Era

Chapter Five

As my disorder grew and worsened I became a very angry fourteen year old who very quickly lost my temper. I got out of control easily, very unlike the quiet little girl who always tried to be nice and respectful. At times it got so bad that I would throw things across the room, break objects, and kick holes through walls. I was so mad at everyone: myself for having the disorder, my parents for not understanding and making it go away, the people who constantly made fun of me and did not even know I had a reason for doing these, and anyone else I could think of. I was so frustrated with the thought that this had to happen to me. Why? No matter how hard I tried, I just could not come up with an answer.

All my life I thought that I did not have any of things that other had. I wanted to be skinny, pretty, and popular and I was always the furthest thing from it. Every teenage girl wants that right. I knew that it was okay if I was not like that but most of all I just wanted to be normal. That angered me most of all. I know now that nothing is better than being yourself but at the time I could not imagine wanted to be me.

I distinctly remember times when I got completely out of control and would hit my parents and scream at them and my sister. I would throw myself on the floor screaming, crying, and kicking. I would run out of the house with just my pajamas on and demand to be left alone in the freezing cold of night. My parents did not know how to handle the situation so they yelled back, trying to get me back inside. I began swearing and doing things that I never had even thought about doing before. I could not believe these words were coming out of my mouth. I hated them, but I really hated myself. My sister would tell me that I was ruining her life and I would tell her to go away and leave me alone and then get in trouble for it.

I have always kind of envied my little sister. She has always had the controlled temper in the family, the intelligence, and the understanding, everything I did not have. I wanted to be like her. I hated myself for the person I had become because it was not the real me.

I would run outside late at night and sit at on the cold, hard cement in only a t-shirt and shorts, shivering and crying until my parents came out to bring me inside.

One time I ran into the garage, slipped, and fell on the hard cement, cutting my leg on the water heater. It hurt so bad but I refused help. I always pushed my parents away but I really wanted them to help and comfort me. The thoughts in my head would not stop and I did not know what to do. I felt like I was in a fight for my life.

A few times I contemplated suicide. I wondered if I could do it, if I would be brave enough to kill myself. I thought about how it would be an escape from the hell I was living in. I thought about getting up on the roof and jumping off, but I could not do it. I realized that suicide was not an escape for me. I did not want to give up. I knew in a small portion of my being there was some amazing strength that could get me through this. If I took my life, the disorder would win. I refused to let that happen and I refused to put my family and friends through that kind of situation.

I remember that my uncle committed

suicide when I was two years old. My

parents never told me about it. They just said

he had Cancer and I always believed them. I

was so young that I could not remember what

actually happened. I found out years later

that he had jumped off the Golden Gate

Bridge and drowned. They found him in a

body of water near the bridge.

My mom was always worried that I

was like him. I would get so depressed

sometimes and I guess I reminded her of him.

She used to say that I walked like him, talked

like him, and looked like him. I guess she was worried that I would turn out like him too. She was scared I too, would take my life.

Ever since I found out about my uncle, he has become an inspiration to me. I do not look at him as giving up or escaping his pain through suicide. I look at him as being my star way in the heavens who looks down on me and makes me fight for my life. When I think of him, I cannot give up. I will not do it. I have to stay strong for him, for my family, for myself. After all, I have two life journeys to complete now.

Times became even more difficult and I was such an angry teenager. Most nights after a huge blow out my mom or dad would come into my room and tell me to talk to them and tell them what was wrong. I did not know and I refused to talk to anyone because I did not know what to say. I did not have the faintest idea what was wrong with me. I could not tell them and they could not understand that. My mom would be crying to me and I felt terrible because I couldn't help it and I didn't know what to do. She would hold me and tell me that everything was going to be okay. She promised me that

it would be better but it never was. I was so

confused and I had no idea what was

happening to me. I was not only frightened

but I was losing my patience.

High School Hell

Chapter Six

I remember my freshman year in high school. One of my friends was going to the same high school as me but other that that, I had no one. I have never been big on change so the transition that awaited me was terrifying. Surprisingly the transition went a lot smoother than I ever thought it would. I started to make friends, slowly but surely, that would stay with me to this day. The only problem was that I had this disorder and it was still affecting me.

For as long as I can remember there have been instances where I have been made fun of by other people, mostly those my own age and in my classes in school.

I one time in particular. It was the third week of high school and the freshman were just starting to meet new people and get adjusted when my history class was instructed to divide into groups for class projects. Everybody jumped at the opportunity to work with people they knew, but I didn't know a soul in my class. I ended up stuck with a group of three guys I had never spoken to. From the moment I knew it would be sheer hell. I was shocked with the tension that developed almost immediately between the four of us. We hadn't been getting along well and for some reason these three guys saw me as a potential target for them to shoot insults at. They knew that it bothered me so it made it all the better for them.

We went down to the library and tried to plan out what we were going to do and all hell broke loose (quietly of course). I was getting extremely frustrated with them and one of the three just called me the worst names he could think of. I swear I did nothing wrong. I was simply trying to organize things and finish as soon as possible. I have never been one to start arguments or disagree much so I was shocked with my own behavior when I became so angry with this kid. He made me feel so small and I knew he saw me as "weird." I felt helpless, like I couldn't do anything about it. The little self-esteem I had at the time completely vanished and I thought of myself as nothing more than a loser that nobody liked.

This treatment went on for weeks and I would consistently come home crying. I was fourteen years old and I couldn't handle it anymore. They had crossed the line. I was going through enough crap in my own personal life and I didn't feel like dealing with anything else. The incidents bothered me so much, that my mom called up the school and told them what had happened. They apologized on his behalf and it never happened again.

The experience still rests in my memory and I will never forget what that time felt like.

At the same time this was happening, one of the most popular people my freshman class decided to pick on me for what seemed to be a hobby of his. This person was handsome, athletic, and terribly outgoing. He was the big shot on campus and seemed to have everything going for him. However, when it came to me, he found and a weakness and shot at it. He was in one of my classes at the time and I think it all began when he caught me engaging in one of my OCD rituals. I was obsessed with cleanliness at the time and was terrified of contracting some deadly disease. To prevent it, I wanted to be as clean as possible. He saw me spit on myself, a ritual that in my world, meant prevention. It was something that eased my anxiety and made me feel better.

Unfortunately, he thought it was hilarious. He would laugh at me and whisper to several other people who began to stare at me. Soon he began dropping notes into my locker that resembled love letters. They read, "I love the way you to do this...or say that a thousand times...etc." I would look at the notes and simply toss them into the nearby trashcan, hoping to blend in with the rest of the crowd in the hall. It hurt so bad inside, but it happened and I pulled myself together and vowed to forget about it. I told myself that I just couldn't let it get to me. But, nonetheless, it just kept digging deeper. I didn't want to be around this boy or any of his friends and tried to avoid them at all costs. Of course, only with my luck, he or one of his friends accompanied me to every one of my classes.

An event similar to this happened one day in the cafeteria. Two of my classmates yelled my name and told me to come see them. I quickly walked away, my heart beating a mile a minute. Why the hell did they want to talk to me? I didn't feel comfortable around them and didn't want anything to do with them. Later that day, they harassed me for being "strange" and having weird habits. They proceeded to shove me into the lockers, swiftly walking away as to make to look like an accident. I just walked on. No damage done; only on the inside.

In between all the teasing and stuff I had to deal with as a result of the OCD, I didn't understand why this was happening to me in the first place. It was taking my life away from me and I wanted it back so badly. Teasing, I know, is a part of life, but having a disorder that constantly provokes it is awful.

Reality Hits Hard

Chapter Seven

The dreaded day had come and I was
sitting out in front of my high school
gymnasium. It was about half way through
my freshman year and I was shaking because
I was so nervous. For months I had fought
tirelessly with my parents and refused to go
to a psychiatrist. I had lost that fight and here
I was, forced to submit myself to the shrink.

I saw my parents' green Ford Explorer
pull through the school entrance and my
heart sunk. I had a million mixed and twisted
emotions. I was scared, nervous, and

incredibly angry. I had no clue what was

going to happen.

When we finally pulled up to the

doctor's office, I got out of the car with ease

and just walked in. Why put up a struggle, it

wasn't worth it anymore. The name of the

doctor was etched into the glass door. Near

the door knob there was an unusual keypad,

similar to that of a pay phone. It contained

several buttons and a little knob that had to be

turned correctly in order to open the door and

enter the office.

My parents were given several numbers to punch in and were previously instructed to turn the knob clockwise. The combination was given to ensure the privacy of the patients. I thought to myself, "Privacy? What privacy, the door is made of clear glass. There must be a bunch of geniuses inside." I wondered why it was locked in the first place. You don't see those kinds of locks on the dentist's door. Is this some kind of institution for crazy people? Are they going to lock me in there and leave me all alone? Images from the movies about psychiatric wards traveled through my mind at a roadrunner's pace. Are my parents tricking me into coming here so that I can be shipped off to some foreign place and locked up in a padded cell? The butterflies in my stomach were doing somersaults.

The waiting room smelled funny and was absolutely freezing. I can still remember my spine tingling from the air conditioning. I felt like I was in a meat freezer. The room was a small one with two offices and a bathroom attached. Three uncomfortable chairs aligned the wall and a small table smothered in magazines was shoved in the

corner. On top of the magazines were several

brochures advertising programs that claimed

to stop anxiety, eating disorders, and

depression.

I kept staring at the light switch under

one particular doctor's name printed on the

wall. My mom switched it on and its orange

glow alerted the doctor to a waiting patient.

My mom kept telling me to relax. Are you

kidding me? You try relaxing. The thought

of ink blots and hypnotism kept waltzing

through my clouded brain. I had no idea
what to expect.

Finally the doctor came out of her
office and introduced herself. She had
flaming short, red hair, pale skin, and round
glasses that sat about half an inch off the bride
of her nose. She invited me to come in first
and told my parents she'd talk with them
after. I cautiously walked into the spacious
office area and sat on a large, maroon, leather
couch. It was cold against my skin and small
goose bumps protruded from my calves.
Before I knew what hit me, the questions were

pouring out and I had no clue how to answer them. I tried my best to "explain" to her that I had these exhausting compulsions to do certain things and these thoughts in my head that made no sense but wouldn't go away. I told her I was terrified of death and was scared of getting a deadly disease. I spoke of the times I washed my hands to the point of blistering and changed my clothes more times in one hour than a runway model did in a month. I told her I was always angry and was saying things I never thought would come out of my mouth. I hated the way I felt and didn't know why I felt that way. My eyes were always red and puffy and I couldn't begin to count the nights I cried myself into dreamland. I told her that I remembered curling up in my mom's arms and begging her to make it better.

I kept getting distracted because there was this huge, glittering canvas picture on the wall. It was made of up purple fish and geometric shapes of all sizes. I thought, "Is this supposed to be some psychological test?"

When the questioning stopped, my parents were invited to come in and regurgitated all the information she had

gotten out of me. So much for confidentiality.

I just sat there quietly, desperately trying to

dream of a happier place. It was a completely

uncomfortable situation. The three of them

were talking about me like I wasn't even

there.

My parents told the doctor the same

things I had told them. At that time, the

doctor told me to leave the room and wait for

them in the waiting area. I was so relieved to

get the hell out of there that I quickly

scampered to the door and entered the realm of what I like to call the North Pole.

I still have no idea exactly what was said behind those closed doors that day. On the way home, my parents told me that I had been diagnosed with Obsessive Compulsive Disorder. It was all a bunch of ancient Hebrew to me. My mom proceeded to tell me that the doctor had prescribed a medication called Prozac. I had heard of it on television and I knew that everybody always made jokes about it. It was the "happy drug" for crazy people. I did not want to take it.

The Psychologist

Chapter Eight

The next few visits to her office were a little bit better than the first. I guess she did all she could with me and so she referred me to another doctor who would teach me some techniques to relieve my anxiety. So I reluctantly went over to this other doctor's office, only about a few yards away from the first.

I immediately felt more comfortable in his office. He greeted me with this soft voice that sounded almost drowsy. He seemed okay so far. The first thing he asked me was, "Do you have any pets?" I thought to myself,

" Okay, this guy is all right." I love animals
and at the time I had a dog named Sandy. So
I talked about her a lot and told him that she
was always so loyal to me. Despite anything
that happened, she never thought I was
weird.

Each session get a little easier and soon
he taught me a technique called biofeedback.
I listened to a machine with each phones and
placed two fingers o a "mouse-like" computer
contraption. My goal was to relax enough to
bring the high-pitched noise down as low as
possible. I tried really hard to bring the pitch

down but half the time I failed and half the time it just really irritated me.

That therapy continued to a few weeks and after a while, things started to get surprisingly better. I was becoming less and less anxious and focused more on other things in my life. The rituals were hanging on but it was taking me less time to get through them. I was pleased with how my treatment was progressing and after a while I was able to discontinue my doctor visits. The 20mg of prozac was doing its job for the time being.

However, I couldn't stand the fact that I had to take medication everyday. I worried about having to take it for the rest of my life.

In the beginning, the medication was closely monitored by my parents and they made sure I always took them at the right times.

Today I am responsible to taking my medication regularly and not skipping any doses. At times I forget and am quickly reminded when the symptoms persist and worsen. I have learned to appreciate my medication and instead of resenting the fact that I have to take it everyday, I remind

myself that it helps me function.

Searching For Answers

Chapter Nine

When I was newly diagnosed with
Obsessive Compulsive Disorder, I knew
nothing about it. I desperately wanted to fill
in the gaps so I was left to search alone.
Nobody had actually informed me about
what the disorder was and what it means. I
wanted to know what was wrong with me
and how to fix it.

I read books, personal accounts of
others suffering from OCD, magazine articles,
journals, etc. I searched the internet and kept
an eye out for anything roughly related to the
disorder. I paid close attention to the way

psychological disorders were presented

through the media and quickly became

irritated when I realized the stigma

surrounding these disorders. I was all ears

when Oprah presented her show on "Unusual

Disorders" and imagined how awesome it

would be to meet her.

Researching the disorder helped me to

understand the biological and psychological

aspects but what I really wanted was to talk

to someone else who suffered from it. I

desperately wanted to meet someone who

experienced the same torment day-in and

day-out. But if I wasn't able to meet this

person now, I was certainly going to find as

much information as possible. I wanted to be

able to explain everything that was going on

in my head. The fixing rituals made sense to

me but I couldn't vocalize them in an

intelligent manner. I turned to my journal

and let it all pour out. There, I could express

it all.

A Step Forward

Chapter Ten

Time went on and I couldn't believe it. It was nothing short of a miracle. I was getting better and I was elated. I felt so much better about myself and was generally happy.

Things went all right during the next three years, and although the medication was kicking in, the symptoms were still hanging on. I went in for a check-up every once in a while if something had been particularly stressful. Stress fed the disorder so the less stress, the happier I was. I proceeded to graduate from high school and was ready to go off to college, not too far from my home.

All was going great until I stepped onto the campus. Something about the whole "college experience" didn't quite agree with me. I found that this college was not the right one for me and it was not quite the right time for me to embark on the "journey to independence." I needed to be back home and was determined to get there. It took quite a lot to convince my parents that I was making a decision that was truly in my own best interest, but finally it happened.

I returned back home and began life in the working world. Luckily, I was able to work at two different elementary schools with kids and staff that I adored. I knew immediately that I had found my nitch. I had so much fun with the kids and loved teaching them and playing games with them. My co-workers were wonderful and we had a ball.

Although I adored these kids, I looked at them with envy. I wanted to be one of them; a little girl with no worries, no big expectations, and no big problems to deal with. In my world, I was a failure. I worried so much about taking time off from school and wondered if I would ever have the

strength to continue on with my education.
With all my worries crammed in my brain, I
waited for the next day to pass.

All my friends were away at college
and I missed them terribly. Soon after I
returned from my brief stay at the college, one
of my friends moved to another state to take
care of some serious psychological problems
of her own. I was worried about her and
hated knowing that she was hurting inside so
much. I felt helpless and didn't know what to
do to help her get better. She made suicide
attempts, but thankfully failed, and the

thought of death continued to creep through

my mind. I was terrified that it was coming

back full force.

A Step Backward

Chapter Eleven

At one of my jobs was a young boy who suffered from Leukemia. He was apparently in "remission" and doing fairly well but out of nowhere, the disease was active again. His relapse started the long line of questions, prayers, and mixed emotions. The boy was such a wonderful kid with so much potential. He was so young, only a sixth grader, the son of loving parents, and a friend to all his classmates. I couldn't understand why this was happening to him. He was in and out of the hospital and soon went in for a long stay. He was so sick and there didn't seem to be much hope but I prayed. It was very difficult to face the reality that he might not make it.

My obsessions kicked in full-throttle and the thought of death engulfed every bit of my being. I thought that if I didn't engage in particular rituals then he would die. I wanted him to beat the disease so badly and truly believed he could. This monster inside my head "told" me that if I fixed the scary thoughts and performed the rituals perfectly, than everything would be okay again. It took an unbelievable amount of energy to take on these obsessions each day and each night. My thoughts consumed my entire life and wouldn't go away until I fell asleep. Sleep time was my favorite part of the day. When I was unconscious, I was free.

Many scenarios of "What if?" and "If...then.." floated through my mind and made it their permanent residence. Many times I laid awake preoccupied with obsessions and carrying out compulsions to ease the anxiety. Similarly, the thoughts were just as relentless during the say.

One night I went to my aunt's house, collapsed on the couch, and cried my eyes out. Everything felt so bad. My obsessions were not going away and this wonderful sixth grade boy had passed on. I thought that I should have prayed harder and focused more attention on carrying out the rituals. These are the ideas that "monster" was tormenting me with. I wanted it all to go away. I wanted to be someone else, someone who didn't have to deal with these unrelenting intruders.

I cried for a long time that night and fell asleep depressed and sad. When I arrived home from my aunt's house, I fell apart. My

life was falling apart again and my symptoms

were getting significantly worse. I felt like

my problems were nothing compared to the

boys, but I couldn't fight anymore. I was

weak and needed help.

College

Chapter Twelve

After working one year at both elementary schools, I felt I was ready to go college. I decided to reapply to the University of San Francisco and was accepted into the class of 2004. I was so excited about my new plans and couldn't wait to get back into the classroom again.

However, I was a bit hesitant about whether I would be able to make a smooth transition back into the school routine. For over a year I hadn't been bothered with homework, tests, papers, or final exams and believe me, that was life. But I had to put those thoughts behind me and start brand new.

I was completely overwhelmed the first day of classes and the college campus felt gigantic compared to my small high school. Students and staff filled the grounds, all looking like they knew exactly what they were doing. I had no idea where I was supposed to go and it took me forever to locate each classroom.

Suddenly I felt panicked. Four years felt too long, the work too hard, and the commute too tiring. Each day felt like an eternity and all I could think about was graduating and going back to my jobs where I was happy and comfortable. I wanted to have my life squared away so quickly, but I knew I had to start at the bottom and work my way up.

I declared myself a psychology major mainly because I felt that my life had been touched my OCD. The abnormal processes of the brain fascinated me.

As each day went by, the routine became easier and I began to feel comfortable. I made friends and had fun. Classes progressed and although I was more comfortable, I had trouble concentrating. The symptoms were relentless and sometimes I couldn't even sit in class or participate in class discussions. I missed out on interesting information but forced myself to hang in there and listen the best I could.

I feel that part of the reason I was initially so negative about college was because I didn't want to grow up. I didn't want to have so much responsibility and I knew I wasn't ready for such a huge transition. I was so used to depending on my family, especially when facing the disorder.

My symptoms made me increasingly

dependent on other people and less trusting

in myself.

The Long Drive Home

Chapter Thirteen

Driving was becoming a huge problem for me and is one of the most difficult parts of my day.

I was a commuter student at college and I traveled a total of sixty miles to and from school each day. The traffic was horrible in the early morning hours, and in the midst of it all, I had to deal with a flood of obsessions. The longer it took me to get to school, the longer I sat in the car with my thoughts. When I had nothing to distract me, I performed an endless amount of rituals. In order for the rituals to work, I had to cause my physical pain.

My self-injury started as a way to "punish" myself for the thoughts I had. I felt that if I caused myself enough physical pain, the mental pain would ease and I would be more effective in countering the obsessions. Self-injury quickly became part of my rituals and I ended up hurting myself many times each day. It was an outlet for my extra energy and a way to decrease the anxiety.

Only now do I realize that my self-injury reinforced the obsessions. I had established a new and harmful compulsion that I thought I was helping me.

To put it frankly, I hated driving but I had to do it. It was so difficult for me to sit there and become victim to unhealthy obsessions. I ended up hurting myself and engaging in a fantastic amount of rituals until my arrival at school served as a temporary interruption.

Although I am much better now, I used to get so involved with performing the rituals that I sometimes ended up putting myself and other drivers in danger. At times, I would close my eyes to help myself concentrate and correctly perform a ritual. It was simply an automatic response and I certainly had no intention of hurting anyone.

Along one particular strip of freeway was a cemetery atop a small hill. This cemetery was directly associated with death and the mere sight of it triggered obsessions. I avoided looking at it at all costs.

Throughout the years, I have learned to avoid the things that trigger my obsessions. I have become a professional at diverting my attention but have missed out on a huge part of my life.

All in all, driving was a hassle. I wanted to get to a particular place as soon as I could. I tried listening to music, but the words in the songs triggered obsessions. Almost everything I heard or saw triggered an unwanted thought.

Ana

Chapter Fourteen

Ana is not a person. She is a monster; a monster that fed my mind with lie after life, every day of my life. Ana tried to make me fail, and she won every time.

Ana was created one day in a therapy sessions when I asked my therapist if I could draw a picture. She said to draw what the "monster" in my mind looked like. I proceeded to draw Ana.

I named her after an incredibly annoying professor I once had. She frightened me, insulted me, and simply wore me down. This monster constantly taunted

and tormented me, similar to my obsessions.
Ana lived inside my head and took over my
body. She was my worst nightmare and no
matter how hard I tried, I couldn't get rid of
her. She was tearing my life apart. As much
as I hated her, it was great that I had finally
put a name to the "monster" in my head. I
realized that she was separate from me.
Finally I began to understand that this
monster was a brain malfunction that enabled
the bad thoughts to hang on.

A Miracle on Allie Lane

Chapter Fifteen

Her name is Beth and she saved my life. My mom suggested that I go see her because she knew her from work and really respected her. My past experiences with psychiatrists had not been the best, but I realized I needed help. But she was different. She is a therapist and as nice as they come. Everything she has said to me from that very first day has helped me get my life back.

Beth and I worked on behavior therapy and I changed to a new psychiatrist for medicine distribution and monitoring. I worked hard at my therapy and tried to do everything I could to get better. It was no piece of cake and many times I wanted to give up because I couldn't deal with my condition anymore.

I was evaluated at Stanford University Medical Center and given a long list of medications that might help me. Of those on that list, I've gone through celexa, buspar, paxil, prozac, luvox, anfranil, lexapro, zoloft, and seroquel.

I became very frustrated when the medication didn't work or I couldn't find the right combination, but Beth helped to understand that it was okay to feel that way. She invited me to work on several compulsions including hand washing and checking. Together we made a hierarchy fears, dove into exposure therapy, and practiced relaxation techniques. Many times I failed, but the times that I won, Beth was right there with a big smile. She motivated me to take control of my disorder and to fight to get better. She told me I controlled my treatment and that success was certainly in my hands.

I soon began to work on self-injury and it took a long while to finally improve. I wanted to cause myself pain so much because I thought that if I caused myself pain, no pain would come to others. I cut my face with my fingernails, left scars on my arms, hands, and finger, and banged my head. I felt helpless and the urge was so strong.

Beth taught a technique that helped ease the anxiety. I learned several self-affirmations that assured me that I would never want to hurt someone else and that I didn't really even want to hurt myself. My thoughts were lies and they had to be defeated.

Today I go to therapy once every week and it's the best part of the week for me. I get to see Beth, who has become like a second mother to me. I would never be where I am today without her knowledge, patience, motivation, and love. Therapy is never something to be dreaded or ashamed of. Beth is there to help me and I know she genuinely cares. Sometimes I laugh at sessions and sometimes I cry. She even taught me how to say supercalifragilisticexpialidocious backwards! (Don't laugh, you know you are trying it right now.) She is not only my therapist, but my friend as well and I love her dearly. She has never once given up on me and I know she never will. She is and always will be my miracle, my lifesaver, and my friend.

What Can't Be Spoken

Must Be Written Down

Chapter Sixteen

Writing is a huge part of my therapy treatment. Sometimes it is easier for me to write my thoughts down on paper than to communicate them orally. My journals are my outlet and allow me to express myself in ways I can't in spoken word. Sometimes I write about the day, problems I faced, or pains I've had. Sometimes I write poems, song lyrics, or even draw images. Many times I have written down the obsessions in my head. The thoughts look awfully odd on paper but the point is to bring them out of my mind and onto paper where I can see them as just words.

In past therapy sessions I have kept track on my mood, level of depression, and OCD activity in my journal. I wrote down everything that was going on in my mind and what I felt about them. I had never communicated most of these things to anyone before and I had never them written out on paper.

Writing about my situation is one of the best things that I have done. It forces me to actually look at what is going on inside my head and accept it. Writing helps me to get

my message across to other people. I want

others to understand more about my situation

and learn from it.

A Final Thought

Epilogue

Obsessive Compulsive Disorder(OCD) is an incredibly disabling disorder. Everyday I live with frightening thoughts and images in my mind. But, the important thing is that I have learned to manage it and I have learned so much about how to make my life better.

OCD is a both a biological and psychological illness that originates in the brain. It can impair everyday functioning but can be managed with medication and therapy. Everyday is still a struggle for me and sometimes I wish I could just make it all stop. But I have learned to live with it and put my effort into living the life that I have.

My parents, therapist, sister, friends, and family have all helped me through the tough times. My mom is still there every time I need her and her strength each day is yet another miracle.

As I continue to fight, I have learned that every one of us has problems in life. We all deal with our problems in different ways. However, perhaps the most valuable lesson I have learned is that when there is help available to you, for whatever your problem may be, take advantage of it. Let people help you, learn from your experiences, and love your life. You only have one chance to live, so go out there and live it, and don't ever take a even a single breath for granted. Celebrate the person you are right now. Who knows, maybe you'll learn something.

Journal Entries

1999-2001

January 3, 1999

Dear Lucy,

Well Lucy, I'm fat, ugly, mean, stupid,
disrespectful, loud, lame, smelly,
ridiculous...you could stop me anytime now.
Yeah, you're right. Don't stop me, because I
deserve it. I've got to be the worse person in
the entire world. No wait, the universe. I
wish I lived far away on some other planet so
I wouldn't have to both anyone down on
Earth. Besides, I hate myself. No wonder
everybody makes fun of me at school and
have been for my entire life. I'm a stupid, fat,

ugly, idiot with a psychological problem and

a learning disability. You can't be more

messed up than that. I wonder if I'm gonna

be even more screwed up when I get older?

I've always dreamed of a happy life and

having a job that makes me happy. I've

always wanted to have a family of my own.

But I'll probably end up a bum on the streets,

begging for food or an old maiden with 80

cats. You know who never gets angry with

me? Dillon, my dog. He's the best. I always

seem to mess things up and it's because I'm

too concentrated on the mental rituals. I can't

make them stop. I guess what I'm trying to say in some really whacked out way, is that the damn medicine isn't working. I'm never going to get better. I'm going to be permanently sick in the head, screwed, messed up. I can't control my anger anymore because I'm so frustrated and before I know it, I'm going to be hooked up to that stupid biofeedback machine that couldn't do squat if its life depended on it!

Or maybe I'll be back in the doctor's office and being forced to look at some dumb picture on the wall as the doctor tries to hypnotize me and "deeply" relax me. I hate

them....they aren't helping me. It's not fair.

I'm going to bed now and maybe I'll dream

about something happy. Good night Lucy.

November 28, 1999

Dear Lucy,

Have you ever not been able to

understand yourself. Welcome to my world.

It seems to be what I am experiencing every

damn second of the day. I want to be in

school so badly and I can't wait for this year

to be over. I guess it will help when I take a

class at the junior college in the spring. I just don't understand why the hell I can't be like everyone else. Why do I have to be so anxious all the time?

December 4, 1999

Dear Lucy,

Well, it's been proven. I swear I should be in the Guinness Book of World Records under the title, "The person who has made the most mistakes and never did anything right." Anyway, I was woken up this morning and pretty much yelled at my Dad. I didn't mean too, it's just that when I'm asleep,

I don't have to go through the mental rituals

and I can actually relax. I guess I just got mad

because he woke me up and it took me

forever to finish all the rituals. If I could just

relax and have a clear mind for one second

everyday, I would be eternally grateful.

August 15, 2001

Dear Lucy,

      Today I saw the mountains. Not the small

hills scattered all over the county, but the big

MOUNTAINS! You know, the ones so big that if

you climbed to the top you could see for miles on end. They were so beautiful. I had forgotten what they looked like. I haven't seen them in so many years. It's not just that I saw the mountains, it's the place I saw them from. The dreaded stretch of freeway that I feared forever, served as the sight from which these glorious mounds were seen. I couldn't do it for such a long time, but today, on my way back to my house, I did it. I didn't even close my eyes as I passed the cemetery to the left of the freeway like I usually did. I didn't look away. I knew it would be there. It's always there. It seems like it's there too often. I hate that cemetery with a passion. I hate looking at it because it brings bad thoughts. It serves as an enormous interruption. My mind is always so flooded with horrible thoughts and images and like usual, I got the urge to fix it, but for one single second I caught a glimpse of the mountains. I felt so free and I couldn't believe it. So this is what it is like to drive through the stretch of freeway and actually see EVERYTHING. For one second, I freed myself from the OCD. I can't believe what I was missing all these years. I wondered what it would be like to walk around the world, free of any and all obsessions and compulsions. Perhaps that's what heaven is for. For in heaven you can always see the mountains, and at every moment,

you are free.